...h of the
STREAM
GRAPHICS

FUTURE
TENSE

JONNY ZUCKER AND LEE CARTER

EDGE
FRANKLIN WATTS
LONDON•SYDNEY

FUTURE TENSE

In the last few weeks,
Java French has been able to see
a few seconds into the future.

He is freaked out by this new power.
He has told no one about it...

First published in 2012 by
Franklin Watts
338 Euston Road
London NW1 3BH

Franklin Watts Australia
Level 17/207 Kent Street
Sydney, NSW 2000

Text © Jonny Zucker 2012
Illustrations © Franklin Watts 2012

A CIP catalogue record for this book
is available from the British Library.

ISBN: 978 1 4451 1320 3

Series Editors: Adrian Cole and Jackie Hamley
Series Advisors: Diana Bentley and Dee Reid
Series Designer: Peter Scoulding

A paperback original

1 3 5 7 9 10 8 6 4 2

Printed in China

Franklin Watts is a division of
Hachette Children's Books,
an Hachette UK company
www.hachette.co.uk

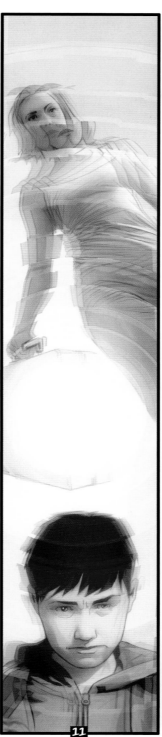

Java escapes on to a train.

Can I borrow your phone?

OK.

Hello, Mum? It's me. I'm in danger. Meet me at the old factory.

He just called his mum...

Mum!

What's going on?

No more secrets, OK?

I promise. I'll tell you everything, but first I think we need to get far away from here...

Slipstream is a series of expertly levelled books designed for pupils who are struggling with reading. Its unique three-strand approach through fiction, graphic fiction and non-fiction gives pupils a rich reading experience that will accelerate their progress and close the reading gap.

At the heart of every Slipstream graphic fiction book is a great story. Easily accessible words and phrases ensure that pupils both decode and comprehend, and the high interest stories really engage older struggling readers.

Whether you're using Slipstream Level 1 for Guided Reading or as an independent read, here are some suggestions:

1. Make each reading session successful. Talk about the text or pictures before the pupil starts reading. Introduce any unfamiliar vocabulary.

2. Encourage the pupil to talk about the book using a range of open questions. For example, how would they feel if they had a special ability like Java? What would the ability be?

3. Discuss the differences between reading fiction, graphic fiction and non-fiction. What do they prefer?

Slipstream Level 1 photocopiable **WORKBOOK**
ISBN: 978 1 4451 1609 9
available – download free sample worksheets from: www.franklinwatts.co.uk

For guidance, SLIPSTREAM Level 1 – Future Tense has been approximately measured to:

National Curriculum Level: 2c
Reading Age: 7.0–7.6
Book Band: Turquoise

ATOS: 1.5*
Guided Reading Level: H
Lexile® Measure (confirmed): 110L

*Please check actual Accelerated Reader™ book level and quiz availability at www.arbookfind.co.uk